THE CELTS

Text: **Julia Drum** and **Harry Sutton**
Illustrations: **Peter Kesteven**
Adviser: **John Reeve**

Contents	Pages
A royal family	2 and 3
The King in his castle	4 and 5
Brion and Maeve	6 and 7
The story of Finn mac Cool	8 and 9
The death of King Gerontion	10 and 11
The King's tomb	12 and 13
Start of an adventure	14 and 15
The cattle rustlers	16 and 17
Queen Brigid	18
The Butterfly	19 to 21
Brion makes his fortune	22 and 23
Starting to farm — quiz	24 and 25
Did you find these things?	26 and 27
Celts at work	28 and 29
Make a Celtic chariot	30 and 31
Brion's Song	32

BBC Books in association with Heritage Books

A Royal Family

Once upon a time there was a Great King named Gerontion, who lived in a palace within a castle. The name of the castle was Place of the King.

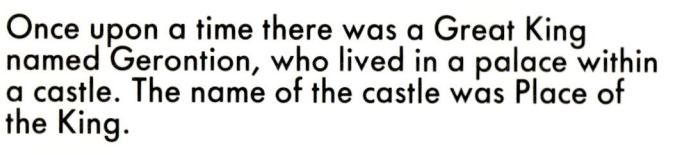

1 The King's castle was, however, really a fort set upon a hill with a high wooden fence all round. For this story is about times long ago, before there were castles with towers and high stone walls.

2 The King's palace inside the fort was built of wood and its roof was supported by tall poles.

3 Even though King Gerontion's palace was not very grand, the King was rich and powerful. He had many faithful followers.

4 The Druids were the most important of the King's followers. They were priests who also decided the laws. The chief Druid at King Gerontion's court was a Prince, the brother of the King.

5 Next in importance amongst the King's followers were the warriors and their families. The warriors were noblemen, and they fought for the King in war.

6 Then there were farmers and the skilled craftsmen who owned land and property. They all vowed loyalty to the King who, in return, promised to protect them from robbers and enemies.

7 The ordinary people of the Kingdom however, were poor. Many of them were slaves who could be bought and sold like cattle. But Gerontion was a good King and there was peace in the lands he ruled.

The King in his Castle

King Gerontion was respected by his people because he was honest and kind. In the summer, when the birds sang and crops ripened in the fields, life was good at the Place of the King.

1 Merchants from distant places travelled to The Place to sell their wares.

2 Only friendly visitors were allowed into the castle. The watchmen at the gates made sure that no robbers or enemies were allowed in.

3 There was always work to be done. The walls of the castle had to be kept in good repair.

4 New homes had to be built and old ones repaired.

5 There were carpenters, blacksmiths, weavers, and many other craftsmen working inside the castle.

6 There were sports, like wrestling.

7 They also went hunting for their food; especially for wild boar.

Brion and Maeve

One day, there was great excitement at The Place of the King. Some important visitors were coming and there was to be a feast of welcome.

1 Meat was roasted over great fires, or cut up and put into pots to make stew; butter, cheeses and fruits of all kinds were collected from the farms all round. Fish were caught and cooked for the feast. At last everything was ready for the King to receive his guests.

2 The important visitors were the family and followers of a nobleman. He was bringing his children, Brion and Maeve, to grow up at the court of King Gerontion. This was how many children of noblemen were educated at this time.

3 'Oh great King', said the nobleman. 'Take my son and my daughter into your care. Teach my son to be a brave warrior, fit to be a nobleman and to serve you. Teach my daughter to be skilful at sewing and weaving as befits the wife of a nobleman.' And so, Brion and Maeve became the foster-children of the King.

FACT BOX

This is Celtic jewellery.

4 Then the visitors were welcomed to the feast.

The story of Finn mac Cool

And so, the two children were left by their parents at the King's court. Their favourite lessons were stories told to them by the Queen. Here is one of them.

One day, in years gone by, Finn mac Cool, the warrior, was hunting with his men in a forest. Suddenly a fog came down and they became lost. Looking for shelter, they came across a house hidden in the forest. The door was wide open and inside they saw a great hall with a fire blazing in the hearth. Beside the fire there sat an Old Man. His back was bent and his grey hair hung over his shoulders. His grey beard covered his knees.

'Come in,' he called to them. 'Warm yourselves by the fire. You are welcome if you behave yourselves!' Finn and his men were amazed that such an old and weak man dared to speak to warriors in this way. But they said nothing.

A ewe was tied up by the door. Suddenly it slipped its rope and walked to the fire.
'You are younger than me,' said the Old Man.
'Please take the ewe back to the door.'
Finn mac Cool took the ewe by the horns to lead it back but the ewe butted him with her head and threw him to the ground.

One of his men then tried but he also was butted to the floor. Several more tried but could not move the animal at all. Then the Old Man got up. 'You are a poor lot, I must say,' he told them as he led the ewe quietly back to the door.

Finn and his men were looking in wonder at this, when the door opened and a beautiful young girl came in with food for them. She was the loveliest girl Finn had ever seen and as she passed he took her hand. But she tore herself free. 'All of you men have once had me in your grasp,' she cried, 'and have thought very little of me.' And setting the food on the table, went angrily away. When the men had eaten their meal, the Old Man told them that beds were ready, saying: 'I'm sure that you are tired after hunting all day.'

The next morning after breakfast, served by the same beautiful girl, Finn mac Cool thanked the Old Man for making them welcome. 'I have three questions to ask you,' Finn told him, 'and I shall be grateful for answers to them.' 'When we came here last night you said that we were welcome providing we behaved ourselves. First, how dares a weak old man like you speak to famous warriors like that? Second, how were you able to move the ewe when we were all butted off our feet by the animal? And the third question is, what did the beautiful maiden mean when she said that we had all once had her in our grasp? None of us, I swear, had ever set eyes upon her before.'

'Those are good questions,' said the Old Man. 'The girl who served you is really Youth, and when you had youth in your grasp you thought nothing of it, wasting it until it left you forever. The ewe is really the World and the World will always be too strong for even the mightiest of warriors. And as for me, I am really Death, and I have everybody on earth under my thumb!'

Before he could ask another question, Finn mac Cool found that the house and the Old Man had gone. He and his men were standing in the forest, with nothing to be seen but trees flowers and birds!

9

Death of King Gerontion

Brion and Maeve were very happy with their foster parents. They grew up together to be strong, brave, kind and honest. But one sad day, the Queen called them to her. She had bad news for them.

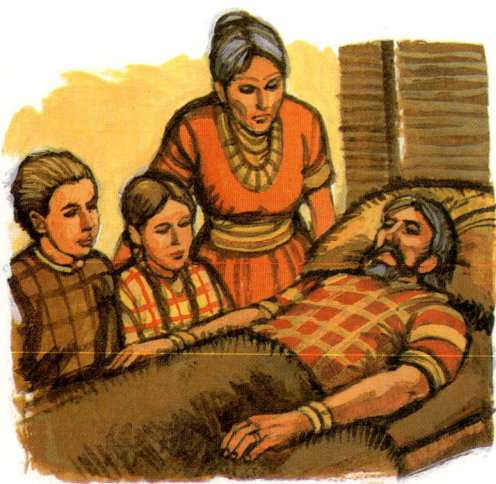

1 'The King, your foster father, is dying,' she told them gently. 'Soon there will be a new King in his place.'

2 As the King lay dying, preparations were being made for his funeral. He was to be buried in a tomb at a sacred place near the castle.

3 The Queen and the children also made ready for the King's death and for the funeral. They believed that King Gerontion was going to the Otherworld and would need all the things of this world for his life there.

4 In the Otherworld, the King would still be a great warrior. He would need his chariot and harnesses for the Otherworld horses. He would also need food and drink. The children were sad as they watched the work going on.

5 The King's followers came from near and far for the royal funeral.

The King's Tomb

In this picture there are 10 things put into the tomb for the king to have in the Otherworld. See if you can find them. The answers are inside the back cover.

Start of an Adventure

One of the dead King's brothers was now King of The Place. He did not want Brion as his foster-son for he had sons of his own. He told Brion that he was now old enough to leave The Place and find his own way in the world.

1 The new King told Brion that Maeve could stay as his foster-daughter for he had no daughter of his own. When Brion had made his fortune, he could return and take his sister home.

2 When it was time for him to go, the King gave Brion many gifts. 'Here is Mac, one of my men slaves,' he told him. 'He is my gift to help you on your journeys, for he is a clever farm worker who may earn money for you. Here also are two of my women slaves. They are each worth two milking cows and they you may sell if there is a need.' Then the King gave Brion a gold coin and some coin bars (see the Fact Box). 'These are the payments made by your father when he brought you to be my brother's foster-son. I return the money to you now to help you in your adventure.'

3 And so, as his sister waved goodbye, Brion set off to seek his fortune.

FACT BOX

4 The road which Brion and his companions travelled along was a ridgeway, used by farmers to drive their cattle and for traders to take their goods to farms and villages for sale.

5 Brion's journey had a good start. He had not gone many miles before he saw a farmer driving his sheep back to his farm for the night. Brion offered him money for a place to sleep, but the farmer was angry. 'We do not need money to give shelter to travellers,' he told Brion. 'You and your servants are welcome to my house as guests.'

6 Brion thanked the farmer. It was, indeed, good to have such a friendly welcome. He would be able to make plans for his journey the next day.

The Cattle Rustlers

Brion and his companions were given food and a place to sleep in their new friend's house. It seemed that their journey of adventure had made a lucky start.

1 Brion slept well after his journey that day, but at dawn he was woken by the noise of shouting and the clashing of swords!

2 Outside, Brion found that a battle was in progress. It was a cattle raid! Warriors from a nearby tribe had come in the night and were driving off the cattle and horses.

3 The farmer had too few men himself to stop the raiders. With Brion, he ran for help.

4 The fort they ran to belonged to a chief for whom the farmer worked on certain days in the year. In exchange for his work, the chief was bound to protect the farmer when he was in trouble. Now, hearing of the cattle raid, the chief called his warriors together. They would find the raiders and get the cattle back.

5 When the Chief's men caught up with the raiders, a fierce battle took place. Many of the raiders were killed and in the struggle Brion was taken prisoner. It was, for a time anyway, the end of his great adventure.

Queen Brigid

Brion and his slaves were marched off by his captors and after many weary miles, they found themselves at another royal castle. This was the fort of Queen Brigid, the ruler of a powerful Celtic tribe.

1 The fierce warriors who brought the captives before the queen, were afraid of nothing in war. But they feared their queen. They showed their respect as they presented their captives to be her slaves.

2 The queen, however, sent the warriors away, then she beckoned Brion towards her.

3 'You have been foster-child to King Gerontion, my old friend,' she told him. 'Therefore, you have learned to live at a royal court. If you live now at my court, how will you repay me if I accept you as a slave?'

4 'I can tell many stories, great queen,' he told her. 'And I can make music with my lute. I can please you with both.'

5 'Let us hear one of your stories,' said the queen.

18

The Butterfly

Once upon a time, began Brion, there were two men, searching for lost sheep in a glen. They were both tired after their day's work. Sitting down to rest beside a stream that flowed through the glen, one of the men lay back and was soon fast asleep. The evening was so fine and pleasant that the other man stayed awake, watching the sunshine glinting on the waters of the stream.

As he watched his sleeping friend, he noticed his mouth opening and out of it flew a pretty white butterfly. It flew along his body and along one of his legs before landing lightly on the grass. It fluttered on for a few yards and the man who was awake rose to his feet. He followed the butterfly curious to see where it would go.

The butterfly flew ahead to the edge of the stream where it stopped for a moment and drank deeply from the water. Then it went on, landing here on a smooth-washed stone; stopping there to drink nectar from a wild flower; flying in and out of the waterside reeds. Then, to the watching man's surprise, the busy insect came to an old horse skull, dry and weather-bleached. The butterfly went in by one empty eye socket and the man watched as it fluttered about, searching the inside of the skull. Then from the other eye socket, out the butterfly came again! It flew back, exactly as it had come. Across the smooth wet stones; around the waterside reeds over the clumps of wild flowers and along the bank to where the other man still lay, fast asleep.

The butterfly never stopped until it flew along the man's leg, up his body and then — into his open mouth. When it did, the man closed his mouth and sighing deeply, yawned and opened his eyes. Looking round, he saw his friend watching him.
'It must be late evening by now,' he said. 'I have had a long sleep.'
'Whether it is late or early,' replied his friend, 'I have seen some great wonders just now.'
''Tis I that have seen the wonders, said the sleeper. 'I dreamt that I was going along a fine, wide road,

with trees and flowers at either side of me, until I came to a great river. Across the river was the finest-built bridge I have ever seen. On the far side of the bridge I came to the most wonderful wood in the world. I walked through it for a long time, until at the end of it I came to a splendid palace. I went into it. There was nobody to be seen. I walked from room to room until I grew tired. I was making up my mind to stay there, when an eerie feeling came over me. I left the palace and travelled the same route home. I felt very hungry when I arrived and then, just when I was going to eat some food, I woke up!'

'It looks as though the spirit sometimes wanders around while the body sleeps,' said his companion. 'Come with me and I will show you all the fine places you passed through in your sleep.'

He told him about the butterfly and showed him the wild flowers, the smooth, wet stones, the clumps of reeds — and the horse's skull. Pointing to it, he said: 'There is your fine palace. The reeds were your wonderful woods and the stones are the bridge you crossed.'

They both of them had seen wonders, indeed!

Brion Makes His Fortune

The queen was very pleased with Brion's story. She told him that she would give him to her daughter, Princess Deirdre. He would be her slave and live nearby so that he could often tell stories like the one he had just told. She would give him land where he could live, and a farm to work so that one day, he could become rich and no longer be a slave.

1 From the fence of her hill fort, Queen Brigid showed Brion the land which was to be his. 'There you can make your home,' she told him. 'And when you have built a farm and can grow food, you shall be a free man.'

2 The first job was to mark out the boundary of the land and build a fence to keep wild animals out.

3 The next most important need, Brion decided, was for the farmhouse. It would be a roundhouse and big enough for cooking, eating, sleeping and all the needs of a farmer. It would shelter animals in winter and be a workshop all the year round.

4 The upright timbers had to be cut from the forest and then fixed into holes dug in the ground. Then the roof rafters were tied into place on top.

5 The house had to be weather proof so that it would be warm and dry in winter. Straw was cut and made into bundles to thatch the roof. The outer wall was first built of 'wattles' — strips of wood woven through stakes — (see the Fact Box) and then daubed with mud.

FACT BOX

Making a wattle and daub wall. The mud dries on the wattle, forming a hard, windproof surface.

6 This is Brion's finished farmhouse.

23

Starting to Farm — Quiz picture

Farmers were important people and Brion was lucky to be given land by the Queen. This is a picture of his farm. Not all of the things you can see would have been happening at the same time. Some is winter farmwork, some is work for the spring and some for summer. They have been put together to make a puzzle-picture. There are twelve different things happening. The clues to them are:

Answers to the quiz are on the next two pages.

25

Answers to the Quiz — Did you find these things?

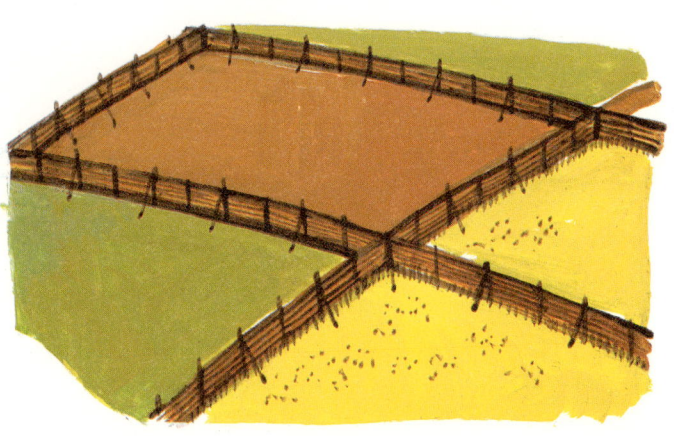

1 Crops growing. Farmers grew crops like barley for making flour.

2 Harvesting of crops. When the wheat or barley was ripe, farmers cut it and left it in stooks to dry.

3 Threshing the grain. When the wheat or barley was dry, the grain was threshed from it so that it fell to the ground. It was then collected and stored.

4 Winnowing the grain. The grain and the chaff of the husks, after threshing, were thrown into the air from a flat basket. The heavier grain fell back into the basket, while the light chaff was blown away. This separated the grain from the chaff.

5 Storing grain in a granary. Some grain, which was needed every day, was stored in a place like this, above ground.

6 Storing the grain. Deep pits were dug and used to store the grain. When the pit was covered over the grain would keep for a long time.

7 Grinding the grain. The grain was ground into flour between two specially shaped stones. They were called 'quernstones'.

8 Keeping bees. Honey was important because there was no other kind of sugar. The bees were kept in hives made of straw and mud.

9 Sheep being milked and sheared. Sheep were important both for their milk and for their wool. Their milk could be made into cheese and cloth was woven from their wool.

10 Pig rearing. Pigs were reared for food but by rooting in the fields, they also helped to keep the soil good for growing crops.

11 Ploughing. The ard was a wooden plough which made a furrow in the ground. The farmer sowed grain in the furrow and after several months this would grow and be ready to harvest.

12 Driving a farm cart. Carts like this were needed for moving heavy things on the farm. They could also be used to take farm produce to market.

Skills — Quiz picture

The people who helped Brion farm were very clever craftsmen, for they had to make everything needed on the farm. In this picture you can see some of them at work. What are they doing? The answers are given on the inside back cover.

Make a Celtic chariot

Things you will need: a detergent bottle top; wooden cocktail sticks; round plastic lid; Plasticine; 12mm dowling; plastic meat trays; 24mm nail; plastic drinking straws.

1 Use the point of a pair of compasses to make 8 holes, equally spaced round a detergent bottle top.

2 Fit wooden cocktail sticks into the holes. These will be the spokes of the wheel.

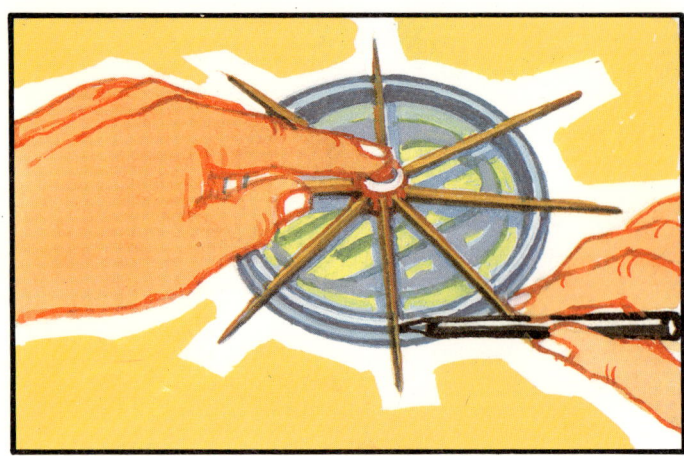

3 Position the bottle top in the centre of a plastic lid and mark each cocktail stick where it crosses the rim.

4 Break off the sticks at the marks. Cut the rim from the plastic lid. This will be the tyre for the wheel.

5 Take a strip of Plasticine. Mould it so that it fits inside the rim like this.

6 Cut the Plasticine into 4 sections. These are the "felloes" of the wheel.

7 Fix the "felloes" to the spokes and fit the tyre round them.

8 Take a length of dowling and cut it to about the diameter of the wheel. This is the axle. Fit the wheel to it with a 24mm nail, leaving the wheel to turn.

9 Make a second wheel and fit it to the axle.

10 Cut the centre from a large sized plastic meat tray. This will make the base of the chariot.

11 Cut other sections from trays to make the sides and front. Fit them together with sticky tape.

12 Use sticky tape to fix the axle to the chariot.

13 This is the finished chariot. Use plastic drinking straws to make the pole in front of the chariot.

31

Brion's Song

Brion went back to the Place of the King to fetch his sister. On the way he sang a happy song. It might have been rather like this song, which has been sung in parts of Ireland for many centuries.

1. I wish I had the shep-herd's lamb, the shep-herd's lamb, the shep-herd's lamb, I

wish I had the shep-herd's lamb, And Ka-tie com-ing af-ter: Iss

O gur-rim gur-rim hoo iss gra-ma-chree gon kel-lig hoo, Iss

O gur-rim gur-rim hoo, Sthoo pat-tha beg dho wau-her.

2
I wish I had the yellow cow,
The yellow cow, the yellow cow,
I wish I had the yellow cow
    And welcome from my darling.
       Chorus: — Iss O gurrim etc.

3
I wish I had a herd of kine,
A herd of kine, a herd of kine,
I wish I had a herd of kine,
    And Katie from her father!
       Chorus.

* The Irish chorus is written phonetically above. Its translation is:

And Oh, I call to thee, I call to thee,
And the love of my heart art thou,
And Oh, I call to thee, I call to thee,
    And thou art the fair child of your mother.